Greetings from
CAPE MAY

Tina Skinner

CAPE MAY LIGHTHOUSE
CAPE MAY, N.J.

Schiffer Publishing Ltd ®

4880 Lower Valley Road, Atglen, PA 19310 USA

Copyright © 2007 by Schiffer Publishing, LTD
Library of Congress Control Number: 2007920203

Designed by John P. Cheek
Type set in Bernhard Modern BT/Souvenir Lt BT
ISBN: 978-0-7643-2678-3
Printed in China

Published by Schiffer Publishing Ltd.
4880 Lower Valley Road
Atglen, PA 19310
Phone: (610) 593-1777; Fax: (610) 593-2002
E-mail: Info@schifferbooks.com

For the largest selection of fine reference books on this and related subjects, please visit our web site at:
www.schifferbooks.com
We are always looking for people to write books on new and related subjects. If you have an idea for a book please contact us at the above address.

This book may be purchased from the publisher.
Include $3.95 for shipping.
Please try your bookstore first.
You may write for a free catalog.

In Europe, Schiffer books are distributed by
Bushwood Books
6 Marksbury Ave.
Kew Gardens
Surrey TW9 4JF England
Phone: 44 (0) 20 8392-8585; Fax: 44 (0) 20 8392-9876
E-mail: info@bushwoodbooks.co.uk
Website: www.bushwoodbooks.co.uk
Free postage in the U.K., Europe; air mail at cost.

Grateful Acknowledgements

This book is drawn from the collection of Elwood "Woody" Koch, who labors throughout the year restoring historic integrity to old homes in the Bloomsburg, Pennsylvania area via lovingly applied paint. Meantime, he counts the days toward his annual weeklong vacation in Cape May. His card collection, featured in part in these pages, helps sustain him through winter months.

Many thanks, Woody and Susan, for opening your doors and allowing us to photograph your wonderful collection. You allowed us in during a trying time of chemo treatments, and we witnessed how the sunny memories of this magical beach resort help sustain you. All who love Cape May are in your debt.

Contents

Overview _____ 6

Beach & Boardwalk _____ 11

Around Town _____ 48

Other Resort Amenities _____ 64

Hotels, Inns & Great Homes _____ 84

Churches _____ 120

Bibliography _____ 128

Overview

The state of New Jersey was first explored in 1633 by British Lieutenant Robert Evelyn who wrote glowingly of a land of plenty, a place so wonderful it was to become known as the Garden State. However, the southern tip of the state, a remote peninsula marking the mouth of the Delaware Bay, drew few white settlers over the next fifty years. Fewer than 700 people lived in the entire county according to the 1726

Every sizeable town and city had a host of these "large letter" cards printed for them during the mid twentieth century. Cape May's can be hard to come by, as this little city is so avidly collected by so many.

Cancelled 1941, $4-7

census records. The highly profitable whale industry drew the first settlers to the area. The high ground offered farming and sites for home building, while a good harbor on the Delaware River afforded easy access to the Ocean. The site was called Portsmouth, New England Village, Cape May Town, and Town Bank. By 1685, the village consisted of approximately twenty log cabins and a tower used to sight whales.

The nation's first Indian Reservation was established by Colonial Government here in 1758, and missionaries began arriving in Cape May and Tuckahoe to save the natives soon after. The area tamed, the cape began to draw sportsman for the fine hunting, fishing, and healthful sea waters. Women soon followed, and boarding houses trailed by luxury hotels were not far behind. The late 1800s were the first heyday for Cape May. A massive fire in 1878 laid much of the new city flat, though rebuilding quickly followed and the city prospered until a more competitive Atlantic City to the north took over as the major tourist destination on the Jersey Shore.

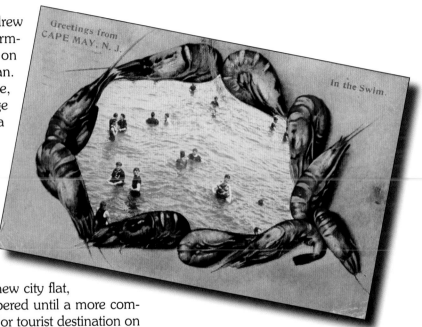

A shrimp border frames "Greetings from Cape May."

Cancelled 1907, $20-25

An aerial view of Cape May, the red-roofed convention center predominant in the foreground.

Circa 1930s, $5-10

Aerial photo of Cape May Point.

Circa 1970s, $5-10

BIRD'S-EYE-VIEW OF CAPE MAY, N. J., LOOKING WEST

THE NEW OCEAN DRIVE FROM CAPE MAY, N.J. TO ATLANTIC CITY, N.J.

COUNTY OF CAPE MAY NEW JERSEY

A bird's-eye view of Cape May reveals one of the town's great charms—a seaside resort where, a mere block from the sand, shade trees shelter sidewalks and beautiful, residential-scale inns and hotels provide an inviting, human-scale streetscape. Cape May provides a sense of small-town America, while accommodating thousands of vacationers each season.

Circa 1910, $20-25

A map details "The New Ocean Drive from Cape May, New Jersey to Atlantic City, New Jersey." Although resorts north of the cape offer more accommodations, often at more affordable prices, Cape May has become a destination for vacationers up and down the shore, even if they're staying much further north. It's known as the "rainy day town" by some, a place where you go on a non-beach day to shop and to marvel at the gingerbread gems.

Circa 1930s, $5-10

9

Cape May languished for years during the early and mid twentieth Century. Its lack of popularity, ironically, played a large role in preserving its treasure of Victorian architecture, which might otherwise have made way for more modern hotels and attractions. In the 1970s, locals in Cape May, the National Trust for Historic Preservation, and the nation at large, rediscovered this gem, and the city has since enjoyed an unparalleled popularity as one of the nation's special places.

This book explores the city's legacy in picture postcards. Postcards were the email of their day, the most popular form of communication at the turn of the century. Then and now, they were considered the most collected item ever manufactured, and because of the popularity of printing, sending, and saving postcard "views," we have a wonderful photographic record of the city as it grew and changed throughout the first half of the century.

Here, for the first time, these images are shared in their full-color glory; printed to accurately reflect the beautiful effect that printers, photographers, and artists created with hand-tinted photographs. Dating and value guides are presented as a helpful tool to introduce new collectors to this affordable hobby, and to help continue the preservation of these invaluable, historic images. For more information, there are several postcard collector societies in New Jersey, and postcard shows held across the United States. More information can easily be obtained on the Internet.

Beach & Boardwalk

First and foremost, Cape May is a beach resort. Loved for her architecture, it is still the sand and surf that draws the crowds. The boardwalk and the amusement piers are inextricably intertwined with her history, and illustrate the city's efforts to attract visitors by drawing them to her beautiful sands and waters.

Beach Ave., Cape May, N. J.

Deliciously open and uncrowded, Beach Avenue is pictured prior to paving. Parked cars and crowds are absent in this scene, and the streets often looked this way when the main means of transport to the resort were via train.

Circa 1910, $15-20.

Beach Avenue, again shown as a sandy stretch of passage in front of the Victorian streetscape that has been so beautifully preserved.

Cancelled 1908, $20-25

Beach Ave., Cape May, N. J.

Besides asphalt, another missing element along early images of Beach Drive is the utility poles.

Cancelled 1915, $10-15

406768

An overview of Beach Avenue shows the Stockton Bath houses on the right.

Circa 1920s, $15-20

Beach Avenue.   CAPE MAY, N. J.

A hand-colored photograph by Joe Hand depicts Beach Avenue. Hand produced many beautiful Cape May cards, each of which is very collectible today.

Circa 1905, $15-20

Joe.K.HAND.

HAND-COLORED.

Beach Avenue. CAPE MAY, N. J.

Young flower sellers peddle their wares on Beach Avenue.

Cancelled 1910, $20-25

BEACH AVE., AT NIGHT, CAPE MAY, N.J.

Beach Avenue is portrayed at night, the sidewalks and boardwalk alive with strollers.

Circa 1910, $10-15

Beach Avenue and Boardwalk   Cape May, N. J.

An overview of a crowded Beach Avenue and boardwalk shows how vehicular traffic quickly became an increasing presence at the resort in the 1920s.

Circa 1920s, $20-25

Begun as the Juvenile Jubilee and Baby Parade in 1928, this annual exhibition is still an annual tradition on Beach Avenue and the Boardwalk.

Cancelled 1931, $10-12

BEACH AVENUE AND BOARDWALK, CAPE MAY, N. J.

In the early days of beach culture, swimming in the ocean was considered a healthful activity. Men and women bathed separately, each in elaborate wool costumes that kept the women covered from head to foot. Changing into the costumes was done in the privacy of a portable carriage drug onto the beach. Cape May offered vacationers the extensive Stockton Bath House, where they could rent swimsuits and change in privacy. Today, the bath site is home to a motor lodge.

Circa 1905-10, $20-25 each

No. 1257. The Stockton Bath House, Cape May, N. J.

Hotel Stockton Baths, Cape May. N. J.

View of beach, boardwalk, and Convention Hall twenty years later.

Circa 1950s, $3-5

Lineup at Band Concert, Cape May.
Presumably the crowds were gathering
to hear music, but even then, this display
of horsepower attracted onlookers. Such
a line-up of vintage automobiles today
would draw huge crowds.

Circa 1930s, $10-15

A bustling scene at Beach
Avenue and Boardwalk.

Circa 1920s, $10-15

Beach Avenue and the
Boardwalk, even busier.

Circa 1920s, $10-15

Hunt's Pier, the boardwalk and the
beachfront are pictured mid-century,
the Conventional Hall in the background.

Circa 1940s, $3-5

The boardwalk, beachfront, and Municipal Pier.

Circa 1930s, $3-5

The bathing beach and ocean front hotels.

Circa 1930s, $3-5

Bathing Beach and Hotels, Cape May, N. J.

Bathing beach and hotels.

Circa 1930s, $3-5

Cox's Pier and Boardwalk.

Circa 1920s, $25-30

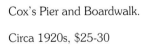

Cox's Pier and Boardwalk, Cape May, N. J.

The bathing beach
west of Cox's Pier.

Circa 1920s, $6-7

Scene on the beach during
bathing hours.

Circa 1920s, $10-15

The bathing beach and Convention Hall.

Circa 1930s, $3-5

Beach, boardwalk, and ocean front cottages "at Cool Cape May."

Circa 1930s, $3-5

Bathing beach and boardwalk.

Circa 1930s, $3-5

Close-up of the bathing beach. Note the transition from beach tents that predominated through the 1920s, to umbrellas.

Circa 1930s, $3-5

Bathing beach and boardwalk looking east.

Circa 1930s, $3-5

General view of bathing beach, boardwalk, and hotels.

Circa 1930s, $3-5

25

Busy day on the Beach at Cape May, N. J.

A busy day on the beach.

Circa 1910, $15-20

On the boardwalk.

Circa 1920s, $15-20

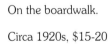

26

Iron Pier and shade tents.

Cancelled 1908, $10-15

Iron Pier and Shade Tents, Cape May, N J

Handcolored

Iron Pier and shade tents. Note the fortune teller's tent in the foreground!

Circa 1910, $10-15

PALMIST

Bathing scene.

Circa 1920s, $10-15

Bathing scene with hotels in background.

Circa 1920s, $10-12

A postcard promotes Cape May. Given away by hotels and businesses, such municipal investments were supposed to create a return in tourist dollars by spreading the word.

Circa 1930s, $7-10

Bathing Beach scene.

Circa 1910s, $10-12

On the Beach, Cape May, N. J.

With Love M.H.B

Early beach scene. This card was produced prior to 1907, when all messages had to appear on the front of a postcard, with the reverse reserved for the address and stamp. Manufacturers often left a white space for messages, and in some cases, people would write across the images.

Circa 1905, $10-15

This card offers a "$5 reward if you find me in this crowd of bathers at Cape May, N.J."

Circa 1910, $10-15

$5.00 reward if you find me in this crowd of bathers at Cape May, N. J.

An early beach scene.

Cancelled 1907, $10-15

On the Sands, Cape May, N. J.

A beautiful hand-tinted beach scene.

Cancelled 1911, $15-20

Busy Day on the Beach at Cape May, N.J.

Surf crashes against the boardwalk in a storm's aftermath.

Cancelled 1922, $15-20

The Fun Factory amusement pier at Sewell's Point was built in 1912. An excursion boat is shown leaving the dock. The viewing platform on the top stood 85 feet above the water. Trolleys brought people to the pier, an ambitious undertaking that helped lead developer Nelson Z. Graves into bankruptcy by 1915.

Circa 1920s, $25-30

219336

CONVENTION PIER, CAPE MAY, N. J.

An early image of Convention Hall, an entertainment pier built in 1917 by the city.

Circa 1920, $10-12

CONVENTION HALL, CAPE MAY, N. J.

The Spanish Revival façade of Convention Hall appears very out of place in today's concept of Cape May as a Victorian town. At the time, however, it was at the forefront of a wave of enthusiasm for the style that swept the nation in the 1920s and '30s.

Circa 1920s, $8-10

Convention Hall Pier   Cape May, N. J.

Commercial businesses were allowed to lease space in the Conventional Hall Pier, and early takers included a pharmacy, a theater, a dry good's dealer, and Ricker's—which, among other vacation essentials, dealt in postcards!

Circa 1920s, $12-15

Dance floor, convention hall. Concerts and dances were an essential part of the vacation experience in the 1920s. Orchestral performances took place nightly, and dancing was both taught and indulged in on this spacious dance floor. Even children got their chance with twice-weekly children's dances.

Circa 1920s, $20-25 each

The Municipal Pier is shown in context, a massive presence overlooking the beach scene. A great pier behind the hall was used for fishing. The pier was damaged by several storms, including the 1944 hurricane that spelled its demise.

Circa 1930s, $3-5

The original Convention Hall and pier were damaged beyond repair by a great storm in 1962. The replacement is massive, but lacking the stylish façade that graced the first.

Circa 1960s, $3-5

The Pier, Cape May, N. J.

The same image, tinted two ways to create day and night scenes of the iron pier. Similar piers being a great draw for competitors, Cape May undertook to create its own iron pier, which opened in 1884. Extending 1,000 feet into the Atlantic, the pier included a band pavilion and dance floor, along with a lower level for sports fishing. It was destroyed by fire in 1907.

Circa 1905, $10-12 each

Nr. 2 — The Surf and Iron Pier, Cape May, N. J.

A beach pavilion in the foreground, the Iron Pier behind it. A separate pavilion on the beach was used as a social center for African-American residents and visitors before desegregation in the 1960s.

Circa 1910, $15-20

The beach front at Cape May, a lifesaving boat at the ready.

Circa 1930s, $3-6

The Life Boat, Cape May, N. J.

The Life Boat at Cape May has been an essential beach appliance since the resort started attracting city dwellers to escape to the shore and take in the healthful waters in thick, wool swimsuits.

Cancelled 1906, $10-15

U. S. Life Saving Station, Cape May Point.

Circa 1920s, $30-35

Someone had fun with this card before mailing it to friends in Pennsylvania. Still, the card offers a wonderful view of the lifesaving team launching the lifeboat.

Circa 1920s, $20-25

LAUNCHING THE LIFE BOAT, CAPE MAY, N. J.

Another view of the Life Boat at the ready. Parasols protect the porcelain complexions of ladies visiting the shore.

Circa 1905, $30-40

Lifeboat in the Breakers. A generic card, regionalized with a local tag line, this card was printed in Germany at a time when few printers operated in the United States.

Cancelled 1906, $10-15

A more contemporary card illustrates the attraction of having trained rescuers at hand in an ocean resort. This card pictures Cape May's Beach Patrol and the First Aid Station and advertises a "Nurse on duty at all times."

Circa 1970s, $5-10

Lifeguards pose outside their station.

Circa 1970s, $5-10

Artists rendering of the
Cape May Lighthouse.

Cancelled 1958, $5-10

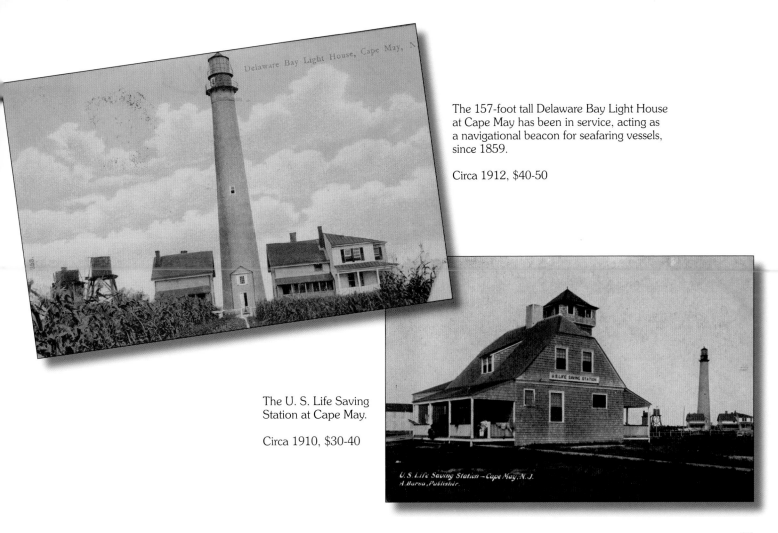

The 157-foot tall Delaware Bay Light House at Cape May has been in service, acting as a navigational beacon for seafaring vessels, since 1859.

Circa 1912, $40-50

The U. S. Life Saving Station at Cape May.

Circa 1910, $30-40

Lighthouse - Cape May, N.J.
A. Barsa, Publisher.

The Lighthouse at Cape May has been restored and operated by the Mid Atlantic Center for the Arts.

Circa 1910, $40-50

A wonderful view of the lighthouse.

Circa 1910, $25-30

The Delaware Bay Life Saving Station at Cape May.

Cancelled 1911, $25-30

Around Town

Cape May is the rare northern beach resort that can lure people out in the fall. The beach-front businesses may close down, but downtown still thrives in the off-season. The reason is the resort's inner charm.

There's still a sense of stepping back in time when one visits Cape May. Much of her architecture is a carefully preserved legacy dating back over 100 years, beautifully framed by old shade trees and underlined with carefully-tended gardens. Cape May is an opportunity to share in the love of community and place. These cards offer a wonderful look back in time, and an opportunity to watch the city grow.

The Boardwalk and beach-front hotels at night. "Linen" was the predominant form for postcards in the middle of the twentieth century, characterized by a textured paper and gaudy color.

Circa 1950s, $5-10

View of Cape May's Promenade.

Circa early 1960s, $3-5

A tractor-like train-pulled trolley appealed to younger visitors during an era when Cape May sought to modernize itself.

Circa 1960s, $4-6

Back to its roots, mules were put to work pulling a trolley for sight-seeing tours of Victorian Settings.

Cancelled 1973; $4-6

Boardwalk strollers.

Circa early 1960s, $3-5

Ocean Avenue in
Cape May.

Cancelled 1906,
$10-15

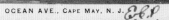

3069   OCEAN AVE., CAPE MAY, N. J.   ILL. POST CARD CO., N. Y.

Beach Theater.

Circa 1940s, $3-5

Beach Theatre and Shops.

Circa 1950s, $3-5

Colonial Beach Theatre
and Stores.

Circa 1960s, $3-5

Washington Street became established as the Business District in the 1920s, its growth illustrated in this hand-tinted, overview photo.

Circa 1920s, $10-15

Washington Str., Cape May. N. J.

Today, anyone visiting Cape May takes a stroll down Washington Street to shop, dine, and enjoy. This early image shows Washington Street long before it became the commercial hub of the town.

Circa 1905, $15-20

A later card shows Washington Street as it becomes even more crowded, still accommodating vehicular traffic

Circa 1960s, $3-5

Washington Street, now closed to cars, is the downtown hub. Outdoor seating, boutique shopping, and the expected beach aromas of fudge and pizza characterize the pedestrian mall.

Circa 1970s, $4-5

An aerial of Ocean Street.

Circa 1920s, $15-20

For those lucky enough to stay year-round, a high school was built in 1901, designed by Philadelphia architect Seymour Davis. A supermarket now occupies this site.

Circa 1905, $15-20

High School, Cape May, N. J.

Columbia Avenue. CAPE MAY POINT, N. J.

JOS. H. HAND.

Columbia Avenue.

Circa 1910, $25-30

Pacific Avenue.

Circa 1910, $25-30

Pacific Avenue, Cape May, N. J.

The beach front in east Cape May.

Circa 1920s, $10-15

Cooley Lilley. From the back: "gifts, greeting cards, toys, come in and browse around. Beach Avenue at Decatur Street,... 703 Edgmont Avenue, Chester, Pa".

Circa 1920s, $5-10

The Post Office.

Circa 1940s, $3-5 each

**KAHN'S UGLY MUG BAR
CAPE MAY, NEW JERSEY**

Kahn's Ugly Mug Bar. From the back: "Located in Cool Cape May, one of the oldest seashore resorts on the Atlantic Coast, now boasts one of the newest novel organizations, the Loyal Order of the Ugly Mugs. Where the United States Froth Blowing Championship is held annually."

Circa 1940s, $5-10

Children at the Beach in a photo by AaronW. Hand, editor of The Star of the Cape.

Circa 1910, $20-25

Children, at the Beach, Cape May, N. J.

A. W. Hand, Cape May, N. J.

Decatur Street.   CAPE MAY, N. J.

Decatur Street.

Circa 1920s, $10-15

Sparkles outline fences and utility poles in this gussied up black-and-white scene of Broadway Street.

Circa 1905, $10-15

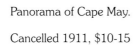

Panorama of Cape May.

Cancelled 1911, $10-15

Other Resort Amenities

Fishing and boating are obvious additional attractions at a seaside resort. Cape May made sure that the gentle folk who came to stay could indulge in pastimes like golfing, theater and music, dancing, and other delights.

What American resort town would be complete without a golf course? For this seaside resort, The Cape May Golf Club fit the bill.

Circa 1920s, $10-15 each

Marine Casino, Cape May, N. J.

Called The Casino, this resort attraction lured vacationers with soft drinks, movies, and dancing—not gambling.

Circa 1905, $25-30

The Marine Casino, built in 1912 on a landfill at Madison and Beach Streets, was best known for its live theater entertainments—suitable amusement for the whole family. Stars who graced its stage included Gloria Swanson and Jessica Tandy.

Circa 1920s, $15-20

406793

A photo card by Aaron W. Hand illustrates sailors enjoying small craft on the bay.

Circa 1910, $20-30

A 443 „Evening" Cape May, N. J.

A. W. Hand, Cape May, N. J.

Both the Atlantic and the Delaware Bay offered boaters and fishermen opportunities. The Cape May Yacht Club was one of many services that sprung up to accommodate sportsmen visiting the Cape.

Cancelled 1908, $25-30

Cape May Yacht Club.   CAPE MAY, N. J.

Another view of the Cape May Yacht Club at Schellenger's Landing.

Circa 1910, $20-25

Schellinger's Landing.   CAPE MAY, N. J.

Boat houses and docks at Schellinger's Landing. Originally developed as a port and shipbuilding center, the landing came to serve recreational purposes when Cape May's industry turned to tourism.

Circa 1907, $25-30

Another view of the docks at Schellinger's Landing.

Circa 1920s, $15-20

Corinthian Yacht Club, Cape May, N. J.

The Corinthian Yacht Club had a distinctive tower to help guide boaters back to shore.

Circa 1920s, $25-30

Sailboat races at Cape May.

Circa 1920s, $10-15

Boat House at Schellenger's Landing. Cape May City, N.J.

Aunt Ella D.

Sailboats anchored at
Schellenger's Landing.

Cancelled 1907, $30-35

An aerial view of Schellenger's Landing.

Cancelled 1947, $3-6

Schellengers Landing. From the back: "We have a darling cottage and the grocery store is only a block away. They sell Abbott's milk. The Bond Bread man and the farmer stopped at our door today. The weather is gorgeous and all the people have wonderful tans. The ocean seems rather rough."

Cancelled 1948, $3-6

Schellengers Landing. Cape May. N. J.

72070

Sewells Point Boat Landing.

Circa 1905, $25-30

Sewells Point Boat Landing, Cape May, N.J.

or" Cape May, N. J.

The Harbor.

Cancelled 1909, $20-20

A montage entitled Sewells Point by local newspaperman and photographer Aaron W. Hand.

Circa 1905, $20-25

Cold Spring Harbor. From the back: "Hello everybody: This certainly is an ideal place for fishing, boating, and bathing. Saw a whole school of porpoises yesterday about ½ mi. from shore. Having a great time."

Cancelled 1928, $30-35

This building was one of the first grand residences , built in 1906 on Beach Drive as the residence of Peter Shields, a Pittsburgh real estate developer. At the time this card was published, the palatial Colonial Revival was serving as the Cape May County Tuna Club. Originally a whaling town, Cape May's introduction to the tourist trade came via men who traveled to the cape to hunt and fish.

Circa 1930s, $5-10

Captain Johnson and his vessel are touted on a promotional postcard.

Circa 1930s, $10-20

Fishing excursions remain a mainstay of Cape May tourism. Here, the Fiesta, captained by Max Grimes, promotes itself via a postcard.

Circa 1950s, $3-5

4 HOUR FISHING TRIPS
ABOARD THE "FIESTA" CAPT. MAX GRIMES
RADIO • LORAN • FATHOMETER   SAILS DAILY—8:00 A.M. TO 12 NOON
DIESEL POWERED   1:00 P.M. TO 5:00 P.M.
PHONE 609-884-4168   FROM CAPE ISLAND MARINA
CAPE MAY, N. J.

The Goose. From the back: "Tuna fishing a specialty, sea bass, flounders, croakers, weakfish, porgies…"

Circa 1950s, $3-5

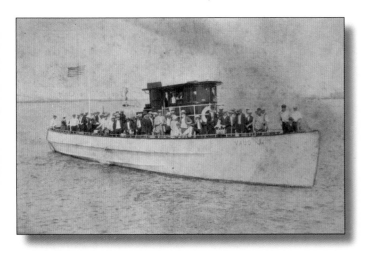

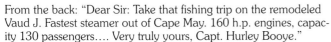

From the back: "Dear Sir: Take that fishing trip on the remodeled Vaud J. Fastest steamer out of Cape May. 160 h.p. engines, capacity 130 passengers…. Very truly yours, Capt. Hurley Booye."

Circa 1920s, $10-20

From the back: "Deep sea and Delaware Bay fishing, the fast yachts Nellie II and the new twin screw Cap Russell…Russell's Dock, 13 Wilson Drive."

Circa 1930s, $5-10

THE NEW TWIN SCREW FISHING YACHT CAP RUSSELL

The harbor fishing fleet. Cape May's watery environment not only catered to tourists, the fish were there for the locals to catch and earn a living from, as well.

Circa 1910s, $15-20

"The Fishing is good at Cape May."

Circa 1950s, $3-5

Tourists came to and traveled from Cape May via water, rail, and roadway. Many piers were built on the cape for the sole purpose of docking excursion boats from New York City, as well as southern ports. Here a card touts the "New Vaud-J II, largest and fastest steamer out of Cape May. 720 h.p."

Circa 1940s, $5-10

CONEY ISLAND.

STEAMBOAT "CAPE MAY" AND DREAMLAND PIER.

Steamboat and
Dreamland Pier.

Circa 1910, $25-30

Cape May Lewes Ferry

An aerial view of Cape May-Lewes Ferry.
The ride itself has become a destination,
with onboard entertainments and the draw
of a few hours on the quaint streets of the
Victorian city.

Circa 1970s, $3-5

The Cape May-Lewis Ferry. The drive from Delaware to Jersey's cape is approximately 170 miles, while the distance by water is only twelve. The quest to establish ferry service resulted in many failures from the first attempt in 1900, through the final completion in 1964.

Circa 1940s, $3-5

The Concrete Ship

"Colonel" Jesse Rosenfeld of Baltimore had a wonderful idea to establish the ferry line between Cape May and Lewes, Delaware. He created National Navigation Company and sold stock to finance his grand scheme, which involved the purchase of several abandoned war vessels.

Cape May came to own one of them: The *Atlantus*. Built by the Liberty Shipbuilding Corporation in Brunswick, Georgia, in 1918, *Atlantus* stretched a full 250 feet in length and 43 feet in width, and had a draft of 16 feet without its engines. Not surprisingly, the concrete design proved too weighty and unwieldy, and the war vessel was discarded by the government after World War I and sunk in the Chesapeake Bay.

The steamer's ill-fated second life began when it was raised from the mud flats near Pig Point, Virginia, in 1926 to fulfill Rosenfeld's financial scheme. Towed to Cape May Point, it arrived on

The Concrete Ship Atlantus has become one of the must-see attractions at Cape May, though it's disappearing slowly. The following images show it slowly sinking through the years. There's very little left above the water today.

Circa 1970s, $5-10

June 8th to await the arrival of two additional hulks that would be cabled to it and run ashore in a "Y" formation, into which the proposed ferry would slip. The final plan was to cap the three half-sunken ships with decking to provide automobile access to the ferries.

However, the grounding took place a little too early. Breaking loose from its mooring, the *Atlantis* struck a shoal and grounded irretrievably. It has been sinking, and breaking in half, since 1926.

Concrete Ship Atlantus, Cape May Point, N. J.

52960

From the back: The concrete ship situated at the foot of Sunset Boulevard was one of an experimental lot of ships built by the United States Government during the World War. The Atlantus was purchased by promoters for use as a ferry landing for a proposed route from Cape May Point to Lewes, Delaware. One night a Northeast Storm broke it from its mooring and beached it and the ferry project did not materialize at that time, but there is still hope that it will eventually become a reality."

Canceled 1954, $5-10

A thoughtfully placed ad on the back reads, "Don't miss the boat insurance, A.M. Blanche." Beachcombers search Sunset Beach for the famous Cape May diamonds. This beach is crowded every evening during the summer as tourists come to watch the sun sink over both bay and sinking boat.

Circa 1960s, $3-5

Excursion boats used to be available for visitors who wanted to row out to explore the Atlantus.

Cancelled 1957, $3-5

The Hotels, Inns & Great Homes

The grand hotels were the heart and soul of Cape May as a seaside resort in the late 1800s. Enormous edifices, they formed the social centers as well as the entertainment for those who made the long, uncomfortable journey via stagecoach or sloop on the Delaware River or via Atlantic to the seaside. The island first promoted itself in Philadelphia, Baltimore, and Washington newspaper ads as a healthful and relaxing escape for gentlemen, who could board with farmers while they enjoyed the surf, fishing, and hunting.

The first hotel in town opened its doors in 1816. It was nicknamed *Tommy's Folly* by the locals, who were convinced this giant venture would fail. The rudimentary wooden structure—which owner Thomas H. Hughes called "The Big House"—featured little embellishment by way of paint and finery. Still, from the first it flourished, and others quickly followed. Crowds, including women and children, began to flock to this seaside spot, and it soon became a summer resort that rivaled Newport News and Saratoga as a gathering point for the wealthy.

"The big events of the each day were the hotel's meal hours," wrote George F. Boyer in his *Cape May County Story*. There were no ice cream parlors, pizza joints, or popcorn stands to patronize in those days.

Those staying in the great hotels, and those who took lodgings in area homes and farmsteads when the hotels filled up, gathered in the hotel dining rooms for the social interaction as much as appetite satisfaction. A great establishment like the Atlantic Hotel might have sleeping accommodations for 300, but seating accommodations for 350 in the grand hall. Guests were seated at long tables, and meals were social events.

Dances were another attraction in the large hotel ballrooms. Bands and orchestras were imported from Philadelphia to perform at formal balls and subscription dances organized by participants.

Other hotel-sponsored activities included entertainments such as shooting and archery ranges, ten-pin alleys, billiards, and other games.

Cape May reached its pinnacle as a resort for the wealthy in the 1850s, prior to the Civil War, which cost the city the patronage of wealthy Southerners. The landscape also changed with the arrival of the railroad and the influx of "excursionists," people who could afford the fare to visit for a day, and perhaps stay a night, though they couldn't hope to rent rooms for the weeks or even the entire season as their wealthy predecessors had.

These hotels were all constructed of wood, since brick and stone were expensive imports. And all were at the mercy of fire—especially the Great Fire of 1878, which leveled over thirty acres of the town then known as Cape Island. In her rebirth, the city changed her name to Cape May City, and a massive rebuilding was undertaken, many of the new homes becoming today's great architectural treasures of Victorian sensibility.

What was reputed at that time to be the largest Hotel in the world, the Mount Vernon was destroyed by fire on the night of September 5th 1856, the proprietor and four other persons losing their lives in the flames. The Dining-Room accommodated 3,000 people.

HISTORICAL CAPE MAY. MOUNT VERNON HOTEL.

The Mt. Vernon was reputed at this time to be the largest hotel in the world. It housed 2,100 guests, and each room was equipped with hot and cold water and gas lamps. The dining room accommodated 3,000 people. It burnt to the ground on the night of September 5, 1856. The proprietor and four other people died in the flames. Postcards such as this continued to circulate years after the hotel burnt down, helping to spread the word of Cape May's role as a great resort.

Cancelled 1919, $5-10

United States Hotel. CAPE ISLAND, N. J.   Destroyed by Fire Sept., 1869.

Front, Cape May, N. J., as it was 50 years ago.

The United States Hotel was built in 1853 on Washington and Decatur Streets. It was destroyed by fire September 1869, too late for firefighters arriving via train from Camden, New Jersey. This image is from a painting, and was in circulation more than fifty years after the hotel burnt down.

Circa 1910, $20-25

"Atlantic Hotel and Beach Front as it was 50 years ago" in a painting by Jos. K. Hand. Leveled by an inferno in 1869, the Atlantic Hotel was rebuilt, and then consumed by the great fire of 1878. The Atlantic was the first Cape Island hotel with a painted exterior. Inside, it boasted accommodations for 300.

Cancelled 1912, $20-30

CONGRESS HALL, CAPE MAY, N. J.

We are staying here for a week.

The original Congress Hall was built of wood, and fell to the flames that swept through the town in 1878. The original three-story edifice housed 100 people in rudimentary lodgings, and was successful from its first summer. It was named Congress Hall in 1828, when owner Thomas H. Hughes became the first man from Cape May County elected to that body. An investment firm purchased the hotel just six months prior to the great fire. On a wave of enthusiasm regarding what fresh energy would do for the city following the fire, the investors rushed to rebuild both the hotel and the pier in time for the tourist season. The new hall was built of brick and placed closer to the beach.

Cancelled 1907, $5-10

nd Boardwalk from Congress Hall Hotel, Cape May, N. J.

The beach and boardwalk from Congress Hall. This institution continues in the tradition of a great Victorian Hotel, offering many luxury rooms updated to today's standards, as well as fine dining. This original Cape May establishment became renown as a summer retreat for the nation's presidents. It hosted Ulysses S. Grant, Franklin Pierce, and James Buchanan on summer escapes. Moreover, it was dubbed the "summer White House" by President Benjamin Harrison, who conducted the affairs of state from his suite in the hotel.

Circa 1930s, $3-5

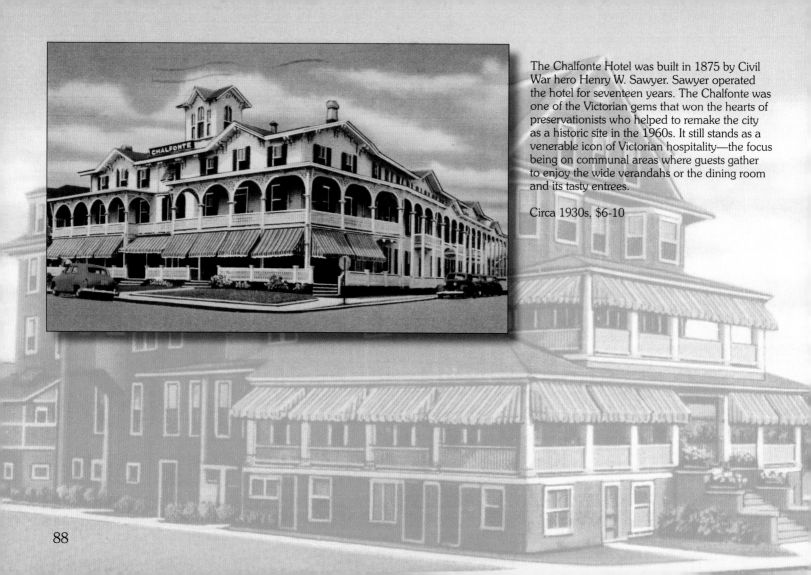

The Chalfonte Hotel was built in 1875 by Civil War hero Henry W. Sawyer. Sawyer operated the hotel for seventeen years. The Chalfonte was one of the Victorian gems that won the hearts of preservationists who helped to remake the city as a historic site in the 1960s. It still stands as a venerable icon of Victorian hospitality—the focus being on communal areas where guests gather to enjoy the wide verandahs or the dining room and its tasty entrees.

Circa 1930s, $6-10

The ninety-room Chalfonte Hotel occupies almost an entire city block on Howard Street and Sewell Avenue. The Chalfonte Hotel escaped the Great Fire, and has been serving up hospitality Southern style since 1876. This great hotel by the sea still retains its Victorian charm—louvered doors to let the breeze through, Southern cuisine in The Magnolia Room, and original antiques and fixtures throughout.

Circa 1920s, $15-20

THE CHALFONTE, CAPE MAY, N. J.

Owners Anne LeDuc and Judy Bartella have worked diligently to restore and maintain the architectural integrity of The Chalfonte, and those efforts that have won them preservation awards.

Circa 1920s, $15-20

89

Hotel Cape May, Cape May, N. J.

Am down here getting fat, comfin'. Hope you all are well. With love Sarah.

An artist's rendering of the Hotel Cape May. The hotel was built amidst massive cost overruns on land dubbed "the New Cape May," and created by offshore dredging to fill in lowlands. It had its grand opening in 1908, billed as being "absolutely fireproof," and is now one of the city's finest hotels. Construction had cost over $1 million. The local press hailed the grand opening as one of the greatest events that had ever occurred in the city.

Cancelled 1907, $20-25

Hotel Cape May, Cape May, N. J.

The scale and cost of the Hotel Cape May made it the talk of the town. This behemoth, designed by Pittsburgh architect Frederick Osterling, had 350 guest rooms. Osterling ended up suing, and winning, $45,000 in unpaid fees from the Cape May Real Estate Company. Within six months, it was clear that the new resort hotel was failing in its attempts to restore Cape May as the shore's leading resort.

Circa 1910, $15-20

Veranda, Hotel Cape May.   Cape May, N. J.

The verandas and porches at the Hotel Cape May were a much-touted feature of the new establishment, and many postcards were produced that extolled the virtue of these sheltered, seaside perches.

Circa 1910-15, $20-25 each

THE PORCH-HOTEL CAPE MAY,
CAPE MAY, N.J.

JOS. H. HAND.   HAND-COLORED.

93

Entrance to Hotel Cape May, Cape May, N. J.

The terraced entrance to Hotel Cape May was another much-photographed feature of the new establishment. The series of steps and overlooks, as well as several patches of carefully maintained lawn and flowerbeds, added an air of elegance to the enormous façade.

Circa 1910s, $10-20 each

ENTRANCE TO HOTEL CAPE MAY, CAPE MAY, N. J.

The Beach at Hotel Cape May.   CAPE MAY, N. J.

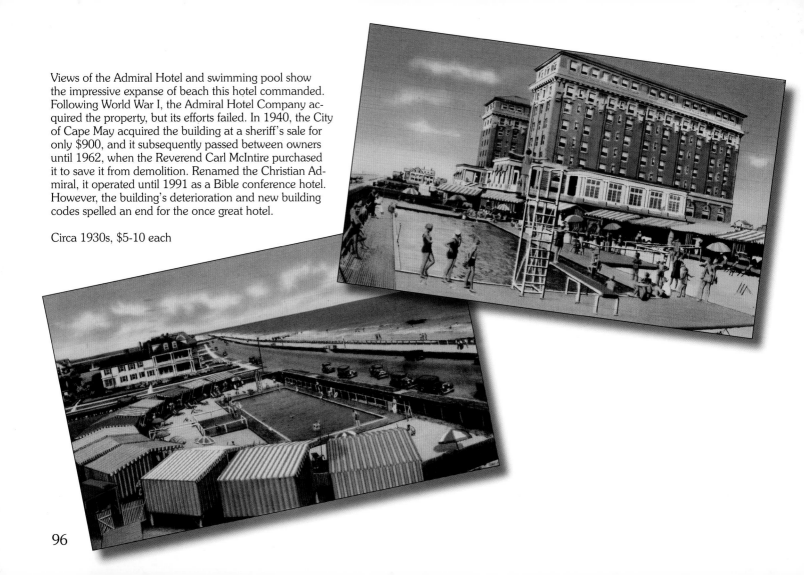

Views of the Admiral Hotel and swimming pool show the impressive expanse of beach this hotel commanded. Following World War I, the Admiral Hotel Company acquired the property, but its efforts failed. In 1940, the City of Cape May acquired the building at a sheriff's sale for only $900, and it subsequently passed between owners until 1962, when the Reverend Carl McIntire purchased it to save it from demolition. Renamed the Christian Admiral, it operated until 1991 as a Bible conference hotel. However, the building's deterioration and new building codes spelled an end for the once great hotel.

Circa 1930s, $5-10 each

THE FAMOUS STRAND AND NEW $1,000,000 CAPE MAY HOTEL, CAPE MAY, N. J.

The hotel didn't find its measure of success until 1963, when fundamentalist minister Carl McIntire bought it and renamed it the Christian Admiral. The hotel became a conference center for McIntire's evangelical reformation movement. The movement ran its course in American politics, and the hotel once again fell into disrepair. It was demolished in 1996.

Cancelled 1907, $25-30

Beach Drive north from a balcony of the Windsor Hotel. The Windsor Hotel was built, in 1868, by iron and bronze foundry operator R. D. Wood. The hotel was destroyed by fire in 1979.

Cancelled 1930, $10-15

Windsor Hotel, R. J. Creswell, Proprietor, Cape May, N. J.

In 1879, Thomas Whitney added two large wings to his existing cottage on Windsor Street and Beach Drive, creating The Windsor Hotel. Architect Stephen Decatur Button added the classic Cape May look with colonnaded verandahs, dormer windows, and a red Mansard roof. R. J. Creswell named himself proprietor on one card, circa 1905, while another boasted about Cape May as the place "Where the Sun Rises and Sets in the Sea."

Circa 1905, $15-20; Circa 1920s, $12-15

The Colonial, hand-colored by Jos. K. Hand.

Circa 1910, $20-25

The Colonial Hotel opened, in 1895, on Ocean Street above Beach Drive. Small by Cape May standards, its matching conical towers gave it distinction. A south wing was added in 1905.

Circa 1920s, $8-15

Colonial Hotel, the bathhouses in the left foreground. From the back: "Arrived here at 2:36 p.m. This is our stopping place. It surely is lovely here Mother. We were down at the beach for a while."

Circa 1920s, $10-15

This Colonial Hotel is now considered a gem of Victorian architecture, but it only escaped the wrecking ball in the 1960s when owner Ray Fite added a modern, fifty-room motor lodge beside the old hundred-room hotel.

Circa 1940s, $5-10

The Hotel Macomber was the last Historic Landmark building erected in Cape May. The shingle-style building was the largest frame structure for its time east of the Mississippi River. Opened in 1918 by Mrs. Sara S. Davis at Beach Drive and Howard Street, this establishment prospered with the wave of friends and families visiting servicemen. A fire destroyed the roof in 1938, and these images reflect the new roof, which came atop an additional floor.

Circa 1930s, $5-7

Hotel Lafayette. This, and the following three cards, show the hotel as she was designed by Stephen D. Button and built in 1885 by Messrs. James and Steffner. The L-shaped hotel was built in 1884 where Decatur meets Beach Drive.

Circa 1910, $15-20

The boardwalk as seen from the Hotel Lafayette.

Circa 1920s, $20-25

Carriage ride concessions in front of the Lafayette.

Cancelled 1916, $8-10

In 1922, new owners Davis and Taylor stripped the Lafayette Hotel of her columns.

Circa 1920s, $25-30

Bathing Beach and Lafayette Hotel, Cape May, N. J.

Bathing Beach and
Lafayette Hotel.

Circa 1940s, $3-5

LAFAYETTE HOTEL, CAPE MAY, N. J.

In 1955, the hotel suffered fire
damage. It has been rebuilt and
currently operates as the Marquis
de Lafayette Hotel.

Circa 1920s, $10-15

105

Sea Crest Inn, Beach Drive and Broadway. The Sea Crest Inn was one of Cape May's smaller Victorian hotels, but the establishment at Beach Drive and Broadway boasted, "Every room an ocean view." Demolished in 1978, it has been replaced by a new Sea Crest that looks every bit the modern 1970s motel.

Circa 1930s, $8-10

OCEAN VIEW HOTEL, CAPE MAY, N. J.

The Ocean View Hotel got its start, around 1850, as the summer home of William Weightman, built at Washington and Franklin. The home was split in two in 1882, and moved to Beach and Ocean avenues, where the local craftsmen found they didn't have the means to reunite the halves—so the two parts were enclosed separately. The Weightman family used the double home until William's death in 1904. Over the next half century, the Weightman Cottage served as hotel, guest house and, during one period, a restaurant. The structures survived the great storm of 1962, but were condemned by the massive rebuilding plan that called for a cinder block hotel on the Washington and Franklin site. Once again, they were moved, this time by a new owner, the Reverend Carl McIntire, who relocated them to their present location on Trenton Avenue, where they were angled to take advantage of the ocean breezes. For twenty years, the buildings were used as dormitories to house seasonal workers and for students of nearby Shelton College. In 1981, they were declared uninhabitable. In 1988, developer John Girton and his wife undertook the massive renovation, investing over three million dollars into turning the property into the highly rated Angel of the Sea bed and breakfast.

Circa 1920s, $10-15

Designed by Philadelphia architects Collins and Autenrieth, the Star Villa got its start as a forty-room boarding house, erected in 1884-85 behind the Lafayette Hotel on Ocean Street. Its initial success warranted quick expansions, and the Villa had 100 rooms to offer by 1887. It was moved to east Cape May in the 1960s, and its original site is now a parking lot.

Circa 1930s, $3-5

The Stockton Hotel was another of the great hotels to survive the Great Fire. Opened by the West Jersey Railroad in 1869, the hotel was considered the country's largest. It filled the block from Guerney to Howard Streets, from Columbia to the beach. It was deemed obsolete in 1910 and was demolished.

Circa 1905, $15-20

The Baltimore Inn opened on Jackson Street in 1893, and served southern families as a seasonal rental. It was demolished in 1971.

Cancelled 1918, $10-15

The Elberon Hotel was one of many hotels in Cape May that boasted of Presidential patronage in the 1800s.

Cancelled 1905, $20-25

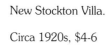

New Stockton Villa.

Circa 1920s, $4-6

The Alcott House, Grant
and North Streets.

Circa 1930s, $10-15

Bellevue Hotel. From the back: Cape May
Court House, 3 miles to ocean, 3 miles
to Delaware Bay, 3 miles to Golf Course,
Open all year."

Circa 1950s, $3-5

Opened as the Arctic in 1874, the hotel's name was changed to Columbia Hotel when Colonel Henry Sawyer, owner of the Chalfonte, leased it in 1890. Later it became known as the Sylvania, and was later demolished. The Ocean Street site is now home to Victorian Towers.

Circa 1920s, $15-20

Victorian House, at 720 Washington Street, is now the restored and greatly expanded Southern Mansion. The grand summer "cottages" of wealthy Southern visitors of the past are the luxurious bed and breakfast establishments of today's visitors.

Circa 1960s, $5-10

113

The Victorian Mansion was built in 1856 by Southern planters as a club house. Today, it is a popular bed and breakfast, shaded by huge trees and difficult to view in its entirety.

Circa 1950s, $3-5

Colonial Cottage, Washington Street, hand-colored by Jos. K. Hand. A cottage is what wealthy individuals called their summer homes—no matter their size.

Cancelled 1910, $20-25

Colonial Cottage, Washington Street.   CAPE MAY, N. J.

JOS. K. HAND.   HAND COLORED.

114

Two cards depict the popular Pink House, one of the city's most photographed sites.

Circa 1950s-60s, $3-5 each

The Emlen Physick Estate is shown during its restoration by the Mid-Atlantic Center for the Arts. This wonderful structure has become a Mecca for aficionados of architecture, as eminent Philadelphia architect Frank Furness has been credited with its design. The importance of this building helped to establish Cape May's role as a noteworthy historic district.

Circa 1970s, $4-5

Atlantic Terrace, Cape May, N. J.

Atlantic Terrace, now called
the Seven Sisters.

Circa 1910, $25-30

Promotional card for The Abbey. "Elegant guest accommodations and breakfast amid Victorian antiques in Cape May's finest Gothic Revival villa." The restored mansion now serves as a seven-room bed and breakfast, its tower a dominant presence on Gurney Street.

Circa 1960s, $4-5

Churches

Though the county's first religious congregation in 1712 with a group of thirty-six Baptists, Cape Island was still too remote for anything but meetings in homes. Prior to the 1840s, the nearest service was at Cold Spring, where a Presbyterian Church welcomed many famous visitors among its regular parishioners. In the 1840s, with the influx of tourists and the growth of the local population, congregations for Methodists, Baptists, Roman Catholics, and Presbyterians were established in the town.

One hundred years ago, it wouldn't have been seemly to take an extravagant trip to the shore simply for fun. The health benefits of the seaside air and dips in the ocean justified such trips in the minds of our forefathers. Attending church services, likewise, was a proper activity for those away from home. For some, however, a simple Sunday service didn't suffice.

One wealthy Philadelphian, Alexander Whilldin, felt that the Cape Island resort offered little in the way of spiritual advancement, and viewed the high life there with disdain.

In Whilldin's time, a widespread culture centered around the Camp Meetings, when families could go on retreat for their spiritual advancement. This was an opportunity for people who lived remotely—farmers and fishermen—to find community within a proper, condoned, religious gathering.

Whilldin was married into the Stites family, which owned what is now Cape May Point. With a vision for a proper moral and religious seaside resort, Whilldin joined forces with merchant magnate John Wannamaker and architect James Sidney to create the Sea Grove Association in 1872, and subsequently launched a new community in New Jersey. The 250-acre site on the point was carved up into 981 building lots all radiating from a central pavilion. The pavilion was designed to seat 2,000, and represented the traditional meeting grove around which the faithful could pitch tents and meet for worship.

In town, churches grew to serve various congregations. Their beautiful edifices still serve the faithful, as well as beautifying the streetscapes of this lovely town.

Ye Olde Church of the Advent
Cape May, N. J.

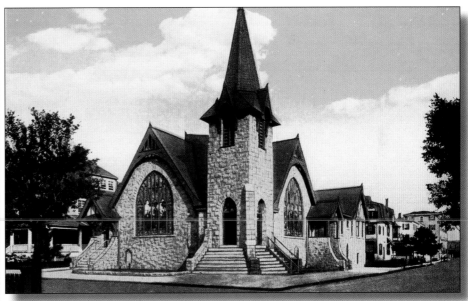

The Cape Island Presbyterian Church at Hughes and Decatur was designed by architect Isaac Purcell. The first services were held in 1899. It later changed its name to First Presbyterian Church of Cape May.

Circa 1920s, $15-20

Ye Olde Church of the Advent was built on Lafayette Street in 1853, when the local congregation broke away from the mother church at Cold Spring. They moved to a larger accommodation, Cape Island Presbyterian at Hughes and Decatur, in 1899, and the Episcopalians soon took up residence.

Circa 1930s, $5-10

Architect George Lovatt designed this 500-seat Romanesque Revival church on the corner of Washington and Ocean streets to replace the smaller St. Mary's Church (which was moved to Lafayette Street). It is one of Cape May's more ambitious architectural statements, built in 1911.

Circa 1930s, $5-7

An earlier image of the Church of Our Lady R. S., Star of the Sea before her ivy covering, which has since been removed

Circa 1920s, $10-12

The Cape Island Baptist Church congregation left a smaller wooden church built in 1879 for this Spanish Revival-style building in 1916. A Soldier's and Sailors' Monument in the foreground was dedicated by the GAR and the Progressive League in 1923.

Circa 1920s, $15-20

The original meeting hall became a Sunday school, and the church was added in 1923.

Circa 1930s, $4-6

The Gingerbread Church, St. Peter's by the Sea. "Episcopal Church, founded in 1880, is one of the original buildings of the Centennial Exposition of 1876 held in Philadelphia. Services have continued every summer since that time."

Circa 1970s, $4-6

ST. PETERS
BY THE SEA
EPISCOPAL

Shrine at St. Mary's By the Sea.

Circa 1930s, $3-6

When it opened in 1890, the Shoreham Hotel was the last hotel to be constructed in Cape May Point. Since 1909, it has been owned by the Sisters of St. Joseph and was converted into their summer retreat house, Saint Mary's By the Sea.

Circa 1930s, $3-6

The Girls Friendly Society Holiday House was owned by the Episcopal Diocese of Pennsylvania. From the back: "Dear E., This is the house where we are staying…. We have some fine bathing here. Have been every day. We have been out on the ocean on a motor yacht."

Cancelled 1914, $25-30

Living Room, Girls Friendly Society Holiday House. From the back: "I'm spending a week here attending the Friends Conference. I'm having lots of fun… I have been to several dances in the evenings, some of them are folk dances. So far I have heard 11 speakers."

Cancelled 1944, $15-20

Bibliography

Boyer, George F. and J. Pearson Cunningham, "Cape May County Story," The Laureate Press, Egg Harbor City, NJ, 1975.

Jordan, Joe J. , *Cape May Point The Illustrated History: 1875 to the Present*, Schiffer Publishing, Ltd. , Atglen, PA, 2003.

Pocher, Don and Pat, *Cape May in Vintage Postcards*, Arcadia, Charleston, SC, 1998.

Salvini, Emil R. , *The Summer City by the Sea*, Rutgers University Press, New Brunswick, NJ, 1998.

Wright, Jack, *Tommy's Folly*, Beach Plum Press, 2003.